Help Desk
Management
in a week

JACQUELINE CHAPMAN

Hodder & Stoughton

A MEMBER OF THE HODDER HEADLINE GROUP

Orders: please contact Bookpoint Ltd, 130 Milton Park, Abingdon, Oxon
OX14 4SB.
Telephone: (44) 01235 827720, Fax: (44) 01235 400454. Lines are open from
9.00–6.00, Monday to Saturday, with a 24-hour message answering service.
E-mail address: orders@bookpoint.co.uk

British Library Cataloguing in Publication Data
A catalogue record for this title is available from The British Library

ISBN 0 340 849746

First published   2000
Impression number 10 9 8 7 6 5 4 3 2 1
Year   2007 2006 2005 2004 2003

Cover image: Photodisc

Typeset by SX Composing DTP, Rayleigh, Essex.
Printed in Great Britain for Hodder & Stoughton Educational, a division of
Hodder Headline Plc, 338 Euston Road, London NW1 3BH by
Cox & Wyman Ltd., Reading.

The leading organisation for professional management

As the champion of management, the Chartered Management Institute shapes and supports the managers of tomorrow. By sharing intelligent insights and setting standards in management development, the Institute helps to deliver results in a dynamic world.

Setting and raising standards

The Institute is a nationally accredited organisation, responsible for setting standards in management and recognising excellence through the award of professional qualifications.

Encouraging development, improving performance

The Institute has a vast range of development programmes, qualifications, information resources and career guidance to help managers and their organisations meet new challenges in a fast-changing environment.

Shaping opinion

With in-depth research and regular policy surveys of its 91,000 individual members and 520 corporate members, the Chartered Management Institute has a deep understanding of the key issues. Its view is informed, intelligent and respected.

For more information call 01536 204222 or visit www.managers.org.uk

C O N T E N T S

Introduction

Help desks and help lines have been set up in most organisations to cope with problems and questions that arise in respect of their products or services. Many help desks relate to the use of information technology (IT) within an organisation; others are set up as a service to customers who may want assistance with a product or service.

The help desk is often the first, and possibly the only, contact a customer has with an organisation. The manager is responsible for providing a service to customers as effectively as possible. This involves managing people, processes and tools, and having a comprehensive understanding of customer service principles.

Sunday identifies the functions of a help desk, explains how to write processes and procedures. Issues are highlighted along with potential strategies for resolving them. On Monday we look at the human aspect: recruitment training and developing staff. Tuesday reviews the tools you might use to improve efficiency.Wednesday deals with the customer and customer service aspects of the help desk.

The remainder of the week looks at some of the more difficult aspects of managing the help desk: communications on Thursday; and measurement and performance on Friday. Finally, on Saturday, there is a brief look at time management, wrapping up with a few tips on how to keep the service under review so that it keeps up with changes in your organisation.

What does your help desk do?

The first step in managing a helpdesk service is to understand what services are being offered and to whom. This chapter aims to:

- Identify the functions the help desk performs
- Decide what type of help desk you have or want
- Understand who the customers are
- Identify the main issues
- Offer help in the writing of processes and procedures

What tasks does your help desk perform?

Your help desk may already exist or it may be something you have to develop from the beginning. In both cases either you should have a mission statement or you may have been set an objective to start or manage the help desk service.

You need to assess the service you are providing. Use Table 1 on p. 9 to help you. Start by listing the tasks that your help desk performs or what you think you want it to perform. This may include some or all of the following:

- Answering the telephone or responding to emails
- Logging customer problems and enquiries
- Attempting to resolve problems
- Passing problems to specialist areas for resolution
- Advising customers of other services
- Tracking problems logged with the help desk
- Keeping customers informed of progress
- Arranging training for internal staff
- Sending information out to customers
- Reporting to management in respect of the number and types of problems that are occurring

Review the list you have made and ask the following questions about each task.

1. Is this a help desk task or does it duplicate work done by another department?
Some tasks such as answering queries should only be done by the help desk but you may find other departments are handling some of these calls; while tasks are done by the helpdesk because they are being 'helpful' but in reality are the responsibility of another department. In both cases, decide where the work is done best and discuss with the manager of that area how best to ensure that work is done in the right place

2. How well do we do this?

If you are taking over from someone else, you will probably have been told what the help desk does well and what it doesn't. Don't take this on trust; spend a few minutes with each member of the help desk and ask them.

3. How much time do we spend doing this?

Each task takes time – you need to work out how much time each task takes. You can probably do a rough calculation to give you total man hours per day or week on each task but at this stage this is all you need; you'll learn about calculating staff numbers and measuring productivity on Friday.

4. Is it relevant?

Many help desks are set up for a specific purpose and acquire other tasks along the way. If your help desk is new scrutinise the list you have made and ask yourself if it is part of the role you have been given. Reject those aspects that are not relevant. Making changes can make help desk managers unpopular; you should either formalise the arrangements or transfer the tasks to someone more appropriate. Tasks that are not clearly stated are never taken into account when reviewing staff levels, productivity or budgets.

Now that you know what your main tasks are, the next step is to document clearly the service you are providing, then after gaining the agreement of your manager or director, *publish it* (see Table 1).

Table 1

Task – Include a brief description of each task	Is this a helpdesk task or does it duplicate work elsewhere?	How well do we do this?	How much time do we spend doing this?	Is it relevant?
Answer and log calls *Take telephone calls, collect relevant information from caller and input into call logging system*	Yes – other departments take calls, this help desk should be taking those calls.	Phone line is often engaged. Staff don't always get all the information	130 calls per day average 10 mins each (26½ hours)	yes
Book training courses *Collect details of training required and contact training provider for courses, carry out all related admin tasks, payment, joining instructions etc.*	No – this is a personnel task	Booking is OK but joining instructions and follow up get forgotten	About 3 requests a month, 30 mins each	No – we should deal with problems only but some problems are due to lack of training – need to discuss with personnel
Objective or mission statement	To provide a rapid statement and responsive service to all staff in the organisation with problems in respect of Information Technology and other office systems, including telephones, heating, lighting and air conditioning.			

What type of help desk?

The table below describes each of the five levels of help desk
service. Some help desks have features from two categories
and these are usually in the process of increasing or
decreasing the range of services offered. It is not unusual for
a help desk to start at level one and in time reach level five.

Help desk type

Level 1: the message desk

This provides a single focal point for users to call. The call is routed to the
person who is best able to handle/resolve the call. Initially this will be the
decision of the help desk agent based upon defined and agreed
procedures. The agent may log the call, allocate a call number which is
then passed to both the caller and the resolver. The help desk responsibility
then ends.

Level 2: the 40% help desk

This does the same as level 1. In addition the help desk agents undertake
some first level resolution of calls (up to 40%). The type of call is usually
'How do I . . .?' or 'It's broken please fix it'. The help desk also takes
ownership of all calls, monitors each to resolution and reports back to the
caller. They escalate calls to a predefined process and produce
management reports containing relevant call statistics.

Level 3: the 80% help desk

The level 3 help desk does everything that the level 2 help desk does or
may do. In addition they resolve more of the calls (up to 80%), again of the
'How do I. . .?' and 'It's broken please fix it' variety. There are, however,
increasing numbers of requests for other services, which the level 3 help
desk will deal with. They are more active in the problem management

process, highlighting trends and identifying means of prevention. Likewise, in change management they are aware of events as causes of problems and recovery processes.

Level 4: the service centre

The level 4 desk does all that level 3 does but to a higher level of call resolution. They are organised to handle service requests such as equipment procurement, administration, etc. They often have access to monitoring tools which they will use to proactively prevent service problems. They are usually in the forefront of service relationship management, producing service level reports and being involved in service reviews. They may also be further involved in aspects of service delivery such as customer training.

Level 5: the system and service centre

This desk does all that level 4 does with the focus still on service delivery. The main additions at this level of service are that they are far more proactive as a result of service monitoring. They may also have other related responsibilities.

Who are the customers?

It is helpful to make a list of the main customers and the services they receive.

Analyse the list of their requirements and place them in order of importance to see what needs to be done to deliver the service they want (see Table 2).

Customer	What do they want?	Can we do it?
Internal Staff	• To report problems with IT equipment so that out-sourced supplier can respond and resolve	• Yes, call logging and tracking • Need skills to qualify calls to supplier • Need details of service agreement with out-sourcer • Need quick contact mechanism with supplier
Retailer	• Information about the delivery of product to their stores. • To report problems with product. • Technical information about the product. • Availability information	• Yes, call logging and tracking needed • Access to production and delivery schedules • Technical data and access to engineering staff
External customer	• To report problems with the company product and get a rapid answer as to when it will be resolved	• Yes, but we need a call logging and tracking system • Access to engineers and their schedules • Staff trained in customer service skills

Table 2

What are the main issues?

You need to identify the main problems facing you, the manager. Prioritise them and think about strategies for resolution.

Many organisations only look at their help desk when there are problems with it and the problems have reached the notice of senior management. You may have been given this

task for this reason. Alternatively, the new help desk you are setting up may be as a result of complaints about the handling of problems in the past, or you may be doing a health check on your help desk to make sure everything is going smoothly. Whatever the reason there are likely to be some issues that cause you concern:

- Calls aren't answered quickly enough or too many calls are being abandoned
- There are too few trained staff or there are never enough people if the phones are busy
- The staff you have are not very customer aware
- Your customers expect too much from your department

Talk to the staff and customers, find out from them what the issues are. List the issues you have and prioritise them; answering the phone to customers is clearly more important than making sure everyone has a job description. Compare this list with the requirements of the customers. Are there any common areas or conflicts of interest – highlight these.

You should now be able to identify the main tasks you have to achieve and the problems you have to resolve. List them. The list may contain a variety of tasks ranging from training staff to getting new equipment. The tasks will fall into three categories:

- People tasks: recruitment, training etc.
- Process tasks: making sure you are doing things properly
- Tools: making sure you are using them and using them effectively

How can you achieve or resolve these tasks and issues?
The list of tasks may look enormous but ask yourself this question: How do I eat an elephant? Answer: One mouthful at a time.There is no easy answer but the following actions will help.

1. Prioritise
You can't do everything; assess what is really important. Set out to achieve the top three to five tasks and make your best

effort on the rest. As you achieve each one, move other tasks into the top slots.

2. Plan activities to achieve
Think through how you can achieve each important task. Write down what you need to do and in the order you need to do it.

3. Allocate time and resources
You can't do everything yourself, don't try. Decide who is best suited to the task and give it to them. If there is no one, train someone but add the training into the plan.

4. Monitor progress
Don't imagine that these things will look after themselves. Spend a little time each week recording the progress made. If no progress has been made, find out why? Do you need to re assign the priorities?

5. Communicate
Let people know what you are doing and when they will see the results. There will always be the impatient ones but if you have prioritised well, planned thoroughly and told them what you are doing, even they will wait.

6. Celebrate Achievement
Nothing feels better than success as each milestone is achieved. Reward yourself and your team, even if it's only with a chocolate bar.

Writing processes and procedures

A process is a single task broken into the individual parts. A procedure is a summary of what you do to complete an objective and may consist of one or more processes.

However, you will often find that the two terms are used in the same way.

Take the list of tasks that the help desk performs and for each one break it into its main actions. If we take the call handling process, for example, its description breaks down into simple steps and the diagram on page 18 shows the call process for a real help desk, with additional comments for those areas where there are problems.

Work processes are best described by illustrations, and conventional flowchart diagrams are the most practical solution. The symbols in Table 3 are the most common.

As you document each of the processes in your help desk, you will almost certainly see where you can make improvements or where problems lie. The process diagram is a working document. Redraw it until you think it will work for your department. Discuss it with your team. Try it out. If it doesn't work try again. When you have time, it is worth expanding the process diagram. Table 4 shows you how this can be done. Each step in the diagram needs to be analysed and documented.

Symbol	Name	Represents
	Terminator	The start or end of any process.
	Process/Activity	An activity is taking place; a description of the activity is usually written in the box.
	Decision Box	A question or decision that must be made. A 'yes' answer usually exits the box from the bottom to the next process; a 'no' answer exits the box on the right hand side to an alternative process.
	Database	Stored information such as a customer database.
	Document	This represents written input or output to the process.

Table 3

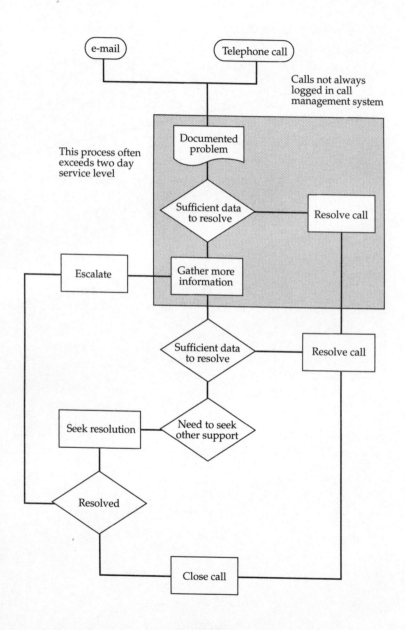

The following table identifies the information required
about each step.

Process step	Who Does It	Detailed Description	Time taken
Answers telephone	Help desk analyst	• 'Good Morning ****help desk. Name speaking. How may I help you?' • Listens to caller, records the following details into the call logging system	approx 1 min
Details logging	Help desk analyst	• Caller name • Caller • Location • Telephone • Type of problem • Details of problem	approx 2–10 mins
Process enters decision box		Assesses whether help can be given immediately and gives it	
Re-assigns call	Help desk analyst	• Assigns priority • Gives caller a log number and a service level • Assigns call to a resolver	
Wraps call	Help desk analyst	• Ensures all information is recorded and service level active • Close record.	

Table 4

This degree of detail takes time but will help to develop processes and procedure that are thorough and efficient. Once each process diagram has been completed, the individuals responsible for each process can be assigned to complete the details.

Summary

At the end of this first day you will have learnt how to:

- List the tasks you perform
- Identify the customers your help desk serves
- Discover the issues you have to resolve and started to think of ways to resolve them
- Begin the process of documenting what you do and how

Hold on to this information – you will need it all later in the week.

People – recruiting, training and managing them

Today we are going to look at the help desk's most valuable asset – the people who work in it. During the day we will cover five main topics:

- The help desk culture within your organisation
- How to identify the skills required by the help desk
- How to recruit the right people
- What are the main training requirements
- Managing and motivating people

Help desk culture

The people who work on the help desk should be your biggest asset. If they are motivated and well trained, you are well on the way to running a successful help desk. Organisations seem to view help desks in one of three main ways

1. The help desk staff are the first step in the customer service function of the organisation. There is a clear role for them and there is structured training and career progression. (This is the aim of anyone setting up a new help desk.)
2. The help desk has evolved over time and the staff employed within it have come from various departments with the express aim of contributing skills from the business to a support function. The staff are customer service-oriented but the role is seen as a secondment from a main career structures. (The help desk is usually successful provided that training is well structured.)

3. The help desk is an 'after thought' that has been staffed by people who cannot be found jobs elsewhere in the organisation. Often, help desk staff are seen as in a dead-end job with no career prospects. There is no structure to either training or career development. (In this case you may have a hard task ahead in both ensuring that the people are trained and motivated, and changing the attitude of the organisation to the help desk itself.)

Whatever the culture of your organisation and helpdesk, as the manager of a service department you have to understand the image your organisation wants to convey to its customers (whether internal or external). In turn, you have to ensure that the help desk staff reflect that image. To do this you have to lead by example, train effectively and recruit the right people.

Skills

Before you can train or recruit anyone you need to know what skills you want. Go back to Table 1 on page 9 you developed on Sunday detailing the tasks your help desk carries out. From each task identify the skills required to carry them out. Some skills will be common to many tasks; others will be unique but essential. The types of skill will usually fall into two categories:

1. Technical or hard skills. These consist of clear and specific requirements. In a software support situation the help desk staff will need to understand the software – how it works, how it is used, how it is configured. Likewise with product support, the help desk needs to know all about the product, whether it is a piece of machinery, or food item.

2. Service or soft skills. These are the skills required when handling customers. They are usually based on common sense and good manners, but human nature does not guarantee that undergoing customer service or other soft skills training will enhance or develop these skills in all individuals. Technically gifted people often find it difficult to cope with people, especially those who don't understand the technology.

A skills matrix, like the one on page 24, is a convenient way of listing all the skills requirements for your help desk. The first column shows the skills required and subsequent columns on a scale of 1–5 determine the level of skill required by help desk analysts (hda) at different levels. A skills matrix will vary according to the needs of an organisation.

How to recruit the right people

How many? There isn't a convenient algorithm into which you can put numbers of problems or calls and be given the number of staff required to cope. To complicate matters, help desk calls never arrive evenly spread out. Depending on the organisation and type of help desk call, numbers run in cycles through the day and over weeks and months with regular very high peaks whenever there is a crisis. On Friday there are guidelines for estimating numbers.

Where from? There are several options open to the help desk manager but much will depend upon your organisation's recruitment policy, which may include any of the following.

Skills matrix

Skill required	1	2	3	4	5	Comments
Technical skills	1	2	3	4	5	
Widget repair	Trainee		Junior		5	Senior
Customer service skills	1	2	3	4	5	
Call answering			All staff		5	Senior and management
Other skills/compentencies	1	2	3	4	5	
Report writing					5	Senior management

Skills matrix

Skill required	Actual skills available					Comments
Technical skills	hda 1	hda 2	hda 3	hda 4	hda 5	
Customer service skills	hda 1	hda 2	hda 3	hda 4	hda 5	
Other skills/competencies	hda 1	hda 2	hda 3	hda 4	hda 5	

1. Internal advertising

Many people accept any job in an organisation in order to seize new opportunities as they arise. If you have a structured career path within your helpdesk/customer service department, you will attract internal applicants. You will also attract other employees who are seeking change, but only if real opportunities exist.

2. Agencies

Recruitment agencies beat a path to your door, usually charging a percentage of salary as a fee for finding someone. Make sure you have clear criteria for the person you want and make sure that the agency checks the skills the candidates say they have.

3. Local advertising

This is very effective if you need part-time workers. Many parents (often very well qualified) seek work on a part time basis and the hours they want to work often coincide with peaks in help desk call cycles. Part time workers want to be

close to their work place (very useful for emergency call-in).
The use of part-timers is often rejected by organisations but
within the help desk environment they are a very cost-
effective use of resources.

A common fear in the use of part-time workers with
children is how will they manage to cope in school
holidays. Often they have support between themselves,
while many local authorities run play schemes which are
excellent for part-timers (although they seldom cover full-
time hours).

Be creative, encourage job share, take on students to do
simple tasks, freeing up other more experienced analysts.
Work with the rest of your organisation to resolve the
problem for everyone.

4. Graduate schemes
If your organisation has well-structured career
opportunities, graduates can learn a great deal by starting
their careers in the help desk. It is unlikely that they will
spend more than a year in the job but as qualified
individuals they should be functioning effectively very
quickly. It is still important, however, to check their
suitability for the role.

5. Placement schemes
Undergraduates often need to find an organisation in
which to gain work experience. This type of scheme
requires more effort from the help desk manager as the
undergraduate has to write a paper on their experiences.
This means that the placement has to have some specific
objectives in addition to providing the employer with an
extra pair of hands.

What skills are needed?

It is important to recruit the right people with the essential help desk skills, including:

- Customer service skills
- A good telephone manner
- Keyboard skills
- Technical or other skills relevant to the type of help desk you run

People working on a help desk need to be articulate and able to explain things easily. Ideally they should be outgoing and able to make others feel at ease. Use the skills matrix you developed earlier in the day to identify the skills you need in your new analyst.

Write a job description. Each member of staff should have a job description anyway, but it is always a useful exercise to write a fresh one for each new member of staff. It means you keep job descriptions up-to-date and it ensures that any new tasks that have come along are included in the job description. You will find an example of a job description at the end of this chapter. Write an advertisement using the job description as a guide. Check you have clearly identified what you want.

Choosing the right person

After advertising for staff, how do you identify the candidate with the right skills?

1. Telephone interviews

These need to be planned in order to collect the information you are looking for. During the interview the following information should be noted; how the applicants actually answer the phone; how they respond to questions; do they attempt to build rapport with the person they are speaking to; how much information do they gather. All this information can be gained by listening carefully. Identify where training will be required.

2. Technical tests

If your applicant is required to have specific technical skills, you must devise a test that measures those skills and apply it.

3. One-to-one interviews

This is often the only way help desks seem to recruit staff. It is fine for getting to know the applicant but it won't necessarily prove that they have the required technical skills.

4. Group interviews

Observation of how people inter-relate is the main aim here but it needs a skilled recruiter to carry it out effectively. Another way is to introduce applicants to other members of the team at a final interview informally over coffee and then collect feedback from the team.

How to describe the job you have to offer

Organisations often fail here because they paint a picture of the perfect job or the job that they think they are offering. The reality is often unacceptable to the chosen applicant and they are rapidly disheartened and leave. As the manager of the help desk you should understand clearly what your staff do and what opportunities are available. If the reality of the job on offer is poor, it is time to look at the help desk roles and improve them for everyone. Recruiting staff into a job that has not been accurately described costs money.

Training

The effective training of staff is very important.

- New staff need to learn new skills
- Existing staff need refreshers and advanced skills
- New processes need to be learned about
- The organisation will adopt new methods and technologies

To determine initially what is required in terms of training, draw up a second version of the skills matrix shown on page 24. The new version replaces the skill level with the names or job titles of each member of staff and then records the level at which their skill lies. By comparing this with the first matrix, the training requirements of each staff member can be determined. If a level of urgency is assigned to the acquisition of individual skills, a comprehensive training plan for the team can be drawn up.

Training methods vary but the most common is known as 'Sitting with Nellie' where someone with the required skill passes it on to someone else by example. For basic call handling this, combined with the use of recording

technology that allows the trainer to listen in and correct
mistakes, is probably the most effective way. Technical
training is often based around a formal training course in a
classroom environment, followed up by hands-on
experience.

Customer service training is often neglected as it is assumed
that because an individual is comfortable with the
telephone and is 'nice to people', they are customer focused.
Customer service training teaches staff how to manage
resources as well as people; good service requires the
operator to be able to say 'no' without upsetting the
customer. Handling angry or distressed people is stressful.
There are organisations which run customer service training
courses and some useful contact numbers are included at
the end of the book.

Managing and motivating people
Job improvement
If it is possible to develop a career structure that shows the
routes into and out of the help desk, this should be done. If
this is not possible, the manager of the help desk has to
ensure that the job is varied and interesting, and that it can
play a part in a career structure with an acceptance that
staff will move on regularly. Putting variety into a job that
follows a similar pattern every day is a challenge and will
require techniques that either encourage competition –'call
handler of the week' – or develops relationships – 'the last
Thursday in the month is curry night'.

Day-to-day management
Lack of day-to-day management usually means that the
help desk seldom achieves anything. There are a number of
management activities that set a routine for all staff, but on
a daily basis you should take the time to monitor call
taking, see how busy the desk is and speak to each member
of staff about the day. If the desk is quiet, ensure there are
other tasks to occupy the team; if it is very busy, make sure
everyone is working on the right thing.

Objective setting
In a help desk objectives are usually more performance-
related than project-based, but it is important to include
both. Performance-based objectives include setting targets
for the number of calls to be taken and the length of time to
be spent on each call. The quality measurements include
assessing the number of re-opened calls and customer
satisfaction data. Objectives that are set need to have the
following characteristics:

- They must challenge the individual
- They should have a clear purpose either through improvement to the individual or the department
- They should be measurable
- They should have timescales attached
- They should be attainable – it is pointless setting something that will never be achieved

Objectives should be reviewed regularly and should be in line with what the organisation wants to achieve. One of the main benefits of setting clear objectives is the clarity of purpose that it gives to the role. Objectives can be tailored to individuals allowing growth in terms of skills. The help desk may be constrained in terms of the range of functions it carries out but there are inevitably extra tasks that need to be done. By allocating these tasks to different members of staff, it is possible to enhance the basic role.

Appraisals
Your organisation probably has an appraisal process but if it does not, it is worth spending time with each member of staff to discuss their progress within the department. If the appraisal process is used effectively good work can be rewarded, and shortcomings addressed before they become major problems. The appraisal should look at each objective and discuss the achievements and progress made.

Discipline
Your organisation will have its own procedure for dealing with disciplinary issues and you should make yourself familiar with it. Minor issues will be left for you to deal with. Occasional lateness is not a problem;

habitual latecoming is. The individual needs to be made aware there is a problem before you resort to a formal process. Most organisations have unwritten codes of conduct in respect of language and dress; a quiet word is usually all that is necessary for someone to modify their behaviour.

Harassment
Any sort of harassment needs to be stopped if seen, and complaints about harassment need to be taken seriously. Help desk staff are vulnerable to harassment from some customers, so make sure you and your staff understand how to deal with it. Such harassment is often abusive. Develop a signalling mechanism that allows you to take over the call or listen in. Advise the caller that you will be taking action against their behaviour and, if necessary, terminate the call. Make sure you are aware of your organisation's policy on all types of harassment and discrimination

Dealing with problems outside of work
People have all kinds of problems to deal with – many come to work despite coping with sickness in the family, divorce, bereavement, debt, wayward children, for example. Most of the time you won't know what the problem is, but sometimes you may be the only person who the individual feels they can talk to. Sometimes all you need to do is listen. Occasionally, the individual is seeking help that you are probably not qualified to give. When dealing with personal problems:

- Use your HR department if you have one – they will often have access to counsellors and other agencies
- Keep a list of useful addresses to hand – Citizens Advice Bureau, Cruse, Samaritans. Be prepared to make the initial phone call
- Don't try to solve their problems – you can only give support and direct them to those who can help
- Keep their problems confidential unless you have specifically agreed with the individual that you will discuss it with a third party

People's private lives are their own unless they affect the work they or other people are doing.

Redundancy

Every organisation encounters this at some point; don't take it personally. If you have to make staff redundant, use your organisation's guidelines. If there are none, fall back on the last in first out. In this way you will be seen to be operating even-handedly. Often organisations will develop criteria based on performance and discipline, using the opportunity to weed out the less able or the more troublesome staff.

Summary

Today we have looked at recruiting, training and managing staff. You should now be able to:

- Prepare a skills matrix to assess the skills gaps in your team
- Develop a training plan to fill the gaps
- Write job descriptions
- Use some of the assessment techniques described to recruit new staff
- Devise a day-to-day management technique for yourself and your staff

Job description: help desk analyst

Job Title:	Help desk analyst
Department:	European IT Fred Bloggs Ltd.
Reporting to:	European IT Manager
Hours of Work:	Contracted hours (35) between the hours of 8–6 pm, Monday to Friday, excluding public holidays.
Description of Role:	The provision of first line support to all users of IT services within Europe and the completion of any tasks allocated to the help desk as part of the provision of IT services to all employees and contractors within Europe.

Responsibilities:

- Ensuring that the help desk is manned during the defined opening hours
- Ensuring that all calls are answered in accordance with the standard operating procedures* and within the defined service level
- Ensuring that all service tasks scheduled or unscheduled are performed in accordance with the standard operating procedures* defined for the help desk and within the defined service levels
- Reporting on performance on a monthly basis in respects of agreed service metrics
- Completing any other tasks allocated by the European IT manager in a professional and timely manner

- Ensuring that a personal development plan detailing training needs is produced at the annual appraisal and completed in agreed timescales

Key Performance Indicators

- Attendance as defined within the terms and conditions of service
- 95% achievement of all service levels
- 95% achievement of good ratings for customer service metrics
- Completion of personal development plan

Review Period   Annual appraisal with quarterly interim reviews.

Qualifications:

Academic:

- Educated to GCSE level with passes in four subjects graded A–C, including English language
- A working knowledge of French or German is desirable

Technical:

- 6 months experience of Windows N.T 4.0 and Windows XP
- 1 years' experience of MS Office '98, or 2000
- 1 years' experience in use of commercial help desk software such as Remedy or Royal Blue
- Working knowledge of Lotus Notes

Personal: Should demonstrate good interpersonal skills at all levels, be able to communicate clearly both verbally and in writing, and

possess good analytical skills for
the resolution of problems. Must be
able to work under pressure and
without supervision.

*See process documentation on page 18

Tools to make things easier

Tuesday will be spent looking at some of the tools that make life easier. These fall into two main categories, help desk specific and telephony tools. If you are setting up a new help desk or if you need to replace any tools this chapter will be quite useful. The tools in most common use include the following:

- Telephone system including CLI and CTI
- Call Logging software
- Automated Call Distribution (ACD)
- Interactive Voice Response (IVR)
- Call monitoring tools
- The internet and intranet
- Remote support tools

Telephone system

It may seem to be stating the obvious when saying that a help desk needs a telephone system. You should consider that many help desks have evolved from a single phone number using a standard hand set with possibly an answer phone attached and that there are still many help desks that use that same technology.

What is the minimum needed?

- A single number for customers to call
- Hunt groups based on an operator activity algorithm
  – this means that the call is not always routed to the
  first number in the hunt group
- Headsets for all operators – RSI is a real risk if a
  standard handset is tucked between head and
  shoulder while the operator types or writes a
  message
- An-out-of hours answering service with or without a
  message facility

When this system reaches capacity there are at least two of
the following symptoms:

- Customers complain the phone is always engaged
- Staff get very stressed and complain of only being
  able to firefight
- Call quality diminishes
- Number of outstanding calls in the system starts to
  climb
- A voicemail system (if used) ties up a help desk
  operator for most of the day

The options are:

- To increase the number of help desk operators
- To add some resource saving tools to the system
  such as ACD, IVR and knowledge-based call
  systems

The following paragraphs look at these in more detail.
Todays telephone systems now include Caller Line
Identification (CLI). This can be interfaced with other
systems such as your call logging system using Computer
Telephony Integration (CTI). For all but the largest
organisations these options are still quite costly to utilise
but are becoming more commonplace.

Call logging software

In the 'old days' before the PC occupied every desk and
organisations were less customer focused, problem calls
and complaints were written onto sheets of paper or into
books or on Post-it notes. In organisations that had a
mainframe computer, calls were sometimes recorded on a
file on this. Every help desk requires some form of call
logging and handling process but what should you choose
and what benefits will you get?

If you organisation is very small and does not use any
information technology such as PCs, laptops etc and the
number of calls you receive is small (less than 10 each day)
then all you probably need is a book into which calls are
written noting the following details: date and time, caller
name, number and address, description of problem, what
action has been taken, how the problem was resolved, who
resolved it, date and time of resolution, feedback to
customer.

Today there are over 250 commercial software packages
that will carry out this function and all its associated
activities with varying degrees of efficiency. Most

organisations have either bought one of these or developed their own software.

As your help desk evolves its needs change. Software that was perfect five years ago may now be slow and lack the functionality more up to date systems now contain. Most managers reading this book will have help desks handling many calls each day and they will have more demanding requirements than simple call handling. These will include:

- Basic call logging – this is the basic information as described above
- Monitoring of progress of call against service level – this tracks the call against the agreed time to fix the problem
- Call analysis – this looks at the types of call received
- Call measurement – this measures the effort put into resolving each call
- Customer database – this is a record of all the known potential callers and may be developed from service contracts or guarantee documents or staff within an organisation
- Product/asset database – this is a record of all the different products or assets against which calls may be made – when associated with the knowledge database this can give rapid solutions to problems
- Knowledge databases – this is a repository of information to help the helpdesk resolve problems and inform customers quickly
- A web browser function to enable access to the system for anyone in the organisation

- The ability to interface effectively with other business and management systems

List the functions you think you need in your software. By deciding which of these are essential, nice to have or not needed you will build a picture of your needs. A comprehensive list of requirements for an average sized help desk can have up to 150 different components. You should also find out whether your staff have any additional ideas and what future changes in your organisation are likely to affect your requirements. You should also discuss with your IT department the technical and security requirements that have to be met.

Your finance department will tell you what your budget is. If you are in charge of your own budget think carefully about what you can afford.

Armed with this information you can then look at products and suppliers:

1. First of all take a good look at the product you currently use. In the interests of keeping costs down, it is worth looking at your software to see if you can upgrade it, whether it is still compatible with other business systems or whether you are actually using all the functions that it is capable of performing.
2. Review at least four other products within your budget – there are various ways of discovering the products you want to see:

   - Look at the software year book. This lists all the software available
   - Search the internet – you will find some 'free'

software but this is usually very limited in its
functionality
- Calling a specialised organisation that has
  knowledge of products in this particular field
- Ask other help desk managers

3. Ask the supplier to demonstrate all the functions you
   need. This takes time. You will probably need to spend
   at least half a day looking at the product and with a
   more sophisticated system you will spend several days
   looking at the functions of the various packages. Assess
   what the software can actually do compared to your list
   of requirements.
4. Make sure the supplier can install and support the
   product.
5. Ask for references from other customers and follow them
   up. Do not assume that just because the supplier has
   given you references they will automatically be good.
   Customers are often happy with their particular
   installation of the product but a key requirement of yours
   may be less important to them and it may not work. Ask
   questions, visit their site, investigate the product
   thoroughly – you can spend anything from £500–£250,000
   on this software so it is important to get it right.

If you are planning to install an expensive system and your
organisation's IT department cannot help, it is probably
worth seeking help from a specialist consultant who, for a
comparatively moderate fee, will ensure the selection
purchase and installation goes smoothly. Expect to spend
around £1000 a day and anticipate that it will take up to 15
days over 2–3 months for a consultant to select and run a
tender for software. Implementation will add to this.

The business case
The aim of a business case is to calculate the proposed expenditure and off-set it against the benefits or cost savings gained. Most software houses have a business case prepared for their product, don't be afraid of using it but make sure you can align the points they make with your organisation.

The main benefit of effective call logging software is time saving. The faster calls are resolved, the fewer resources are required to resolve them. Intangible benefits such as improved customer satisfaction, that in turn leads to customer retention should also be included but not overestimated.

Improved management information from the call logging system leads to preventative activities which reduce the number of calls thus reducing the resources required.

However this is always difficult to prove because the environment is never static and new problems always appear to replace old ones.

Automated Call Distribution (ACD)

In help desks that handle hundreds of calls each day an ACD is a must. The ACD works by answering calls and holding them in a queue or series of queues until an operator is free to speak to the caller. This ensures that as many calls as possible are answered, that help desk operators receive calls steadily allowing them time to complete each call effectively.

The manager can extract information from the system about

the number of calls received, the average duration of each call, the number of callers who abandoned while waiting to speak to an operator, the number of calls each operator handles. All of this information helps the manager to assess performance and manage resources.

The ACD can also be used to give messages to customers and perhaps then to take away the need to speak to an operator. For example, if there is a system failure of any sort, many people will attempt to report it. If the ACD has been programmed to greet callers with information about the system failure then the caller will abandon the call, leaving operators free to handle calls on other issues.

The ACD needs to be compatible with your telephone system so you will need to discuss your requirements with your telecommunications manager, or if your organisation does not have such a manager then you should speak to the supplier of your telephone system.

As with call logging software you need to decide what functions are required from the ACD. Installation of an ACD sometimes brings about changes in existing processes – go back to your process documentation and ensure that the change is for the better. If the product is not flexible to your requirements it is not the right product for your help desk. Many ACDs allow the help desk to play music during the waiting time. There are two points to make about this; first of all make sure you have bought the appropriate licence to allow you to do this and secondly make sure your choice of music is appropriate, *I'm still waiting* by Diana Ross may not strike the right note.

Interactive Voice Response (IVR)

When combined with an ACD, an IVR interrogates the caller and then assigns calls to the appropriate operator. In busy help desks there are often types of call which arise everyday and have known solutions or require specific expertise. By asking the caller to respond to choices using their telephone keypad the system can then route the call to the most appropriate person.

There are some key points to consider in the successful use of IVR:

- Keep it simple – if you offer too many options the caller will not remember them all by the time they have to make a response.
- Do not set up too many layers of interrogation – the caller wants to talk to someone.
- Make sure that at the end of every option there is an answer and a route out of the system back to an operator.

Your telephone system will have to be compatible to use such a system and justification for the system will rely upon call volumes and available resources.

Call monitoring tools

In some organisations calls need to be monitored for legal reasons, others simply want to monitor calls for quality reasons. If the need for call monitoring cannot be proven then it is likely that your organisation does not need it. However if your telephone system is up to date and the facility is already available, then it is worth using the

technology to improve skills and operator performance.
Once again choosing the technology will rest with your
telecommunications manager and it will need to be
compatible with your existing telephone system.

The internet

There are six main uses of the internet within help desk
environments:

- Receive enquiries from customers
- Marketing of company products
- Bulletin boards which give or exchange information
- The publication of statistics
- The advertising of solutions to common problems
- The use of a web browser to log and track calls by
  the customer and other support resources

The use of the internet is likely to be established if your
organisation is making use of the opportunities the internet
offers. Do investigate the opportunities for integrating the
internet with your call logging system via a web browser,
enabling customers to log calls themselves. If you use an
internet based knowledge database make sure the links
work and the pages themselves are clear and easy to use.

Remote support tools

Most likely to be seen in technology based help desks,
remote support tools allow the help desk analyst to resolve
problems from their desk. The tools involved can often be
used to diagnose and resolve problems with computer
equipment or other machinery driven by software. Some

organisations include software within their equipment which, when problems arise, make the call to the help desk or support organisation advising of the nature of the problem and allows the opportunity for remedial action to take place. Such tools can significantly reduce the length of time it takes to resolve problems.

Summary

After looking at the tools available you should now be able to decide whether any improvements can be made to the technology in use in your own help desk. Remember to make a business case for the improvements you plan to make before investing in the improvements.

Customers – the reason you are there

So far we have dealt with all the resources required to set up a help desk. Today we will look at the main reason the help desk exists – the customers and their problems.

- Who are your customers and what do they want?
- What is good customer service?
- Service level agreements
- Handling complaints
- Communication
- Difficult customers

Who are your customers and what do they want?

On Sunday you made a list of your main customers and the services they wanted (see page 12). Today we will take this list and extend it to cover other aspects of customer service.

Table 5 on page 51 shows the information you need to collect about each of your main customers. If your customers are the general public, include the service details as if they were a single customer.

The completed table should help you to see the services you are providing to each of your customers. The most common problem is that customers have an expectation of one level of service and the help desk has insufficient resources to provide it and this is where service level agreements help.

Customer details	Services required	Third party contract	Service level agreements	Cost	Penalties	Estimate of use	Actual use	Review meetings
Name Address Telephone Main contact Account manager	IT support service Call logging Problem resolution Call closure	Yes	Answer within 5 rings Resolve 40% within 1 hour 60% to third party – resolve within 2 days Close all calls within 4 hours of resolution	Standard service (within IT budget)	None	30 calls per day	Jan 29 Feb 36 Mar 31 Apr 60 May 20 June 33 Av. = 35	Quarterly
	Supply loan equipment Admin only	Yes	Arrange for supply within 24 hours Keep accurate records for recharge purposes	£25 per day	None	3 requests per month	Jan 2 Feb 3 Mar 1 Apr 0 May 0 June 3 Av. = 1.5	Quarterly
This column contains the main contact details of the customer plus the name of their internal account manager, if such an individual exists.	*This column contains details of the service the customer expects. Break each service into main tasks*	*Are third parties involved?*	*What level of service is expected at task level?*	*How is it paid for?*	*What happens if you fail?*	*How much use was predicted?*	*How often is the service really used?*	*How often are meetings held?*

Table 5

What is good customer service?

Customer service is the perceived element that gives some organisations the edge over their competitors. It needs to be quick and efficient to satisfy the consumer. A customer expects the following from customer service:

- It must be quick – if possible they want the answer or problem solved now!
- People who know what they are doing and give the caller confidence
- People who are patient, polite and friendly
- Someone to chase progress for them

It may seem like stating the obvious but these skills do not come naturally to everyone. We are all familiar with the singsong 'Good morning, Acme Products my name is Amy, How may I help you?' but it is the delivery of that line that sets the tone for the whole call. Staff need to learn how to

maintain the routine without sounding bored. If you haven't invested in customer service training think about doing so, especially if you serve the general public.

Service level agreements

Many organisations agree a general service level that applies to all customers; others form individual agreements with each customer. However you choose to do this, it is helpful to have a published service level agreement to set customer expectations. They then know how long something will take and how much it will cost. As the service provider it sets a standard by which to measure yourself.

Where no service levels are published, the customer will set his own standards that will inevitably be more demanding than you, as the service provider, can achieve with the resources you have available.

Setting service level standards requires effort in the first place, but once set up are easily revised. Look at Table 5 (page 51) showing the list of services you provide to your

customers. On Sunday you documented a process for each of these services (look back to page 12).

When you have completed the table, it should help you to see the services you are providing to each of your customers. The most common problem is that customers have an expectation of one level of service, and the help desk has insufficient resources to provide it. This is where service agreements help.

Look at each step in the process and answer the following questions. We can use call answering as an example.

How long does this take?	3 minutes
What resources do I need to do this?	Help desk operator, call logging system
How much will this cost?	Fixed costs + salary calculated into cost per minute × 3
How many times each day will I repeat this?	1000
Are there any special considerations?	No

By calculating the resource requirements for each task and then looking at the actual resources available, you will be able to predict the level of service you can provide. In the above example, you will require the capacity to provide over 51 hours of effort to answer all 1000 calls each day.

When you have done this for each service you will be able to construct a service level agreement similar to the one on page 57. If you have insufficient resources to cope, your ability to provide a rapid service is low and your service levels will reflect this.

Your customers will not necessarily be satisfied with the service that you are able to provide and this is where negotiation starts. If your customer is paying for a specific level of service, you must ensure that it is accurately costed before you enter into the agreement. If the service you are providing comes as part of general service offered to customers, then, unless they are prepared to pay a premium for a higher level of service, you should ensure that they receive the basic service.

All these discussions will focus on your ability to provide the highest level of service for the lowest possible cost. In a busy help desk it is this type of discussion that leads to a review of the tools in place. Understanding what you do and how much it costs to do it effectively takes time to calculate, but is worth the effort if you need to run your help desk to either break even or show profit.

You will often be required to provide a service that relies upon others for part of that service. It is important that you set up a service level agreement with your own service providers to ensure that you are able to deliver your agreed services. For example, if you have to ensure calls are resolved within a working day and you need to call an engineer from a third party to do this, the engineer must be required to resolve the problem within four hours. This allows you time to call the engineer after you have attempted to resolve the call yourself. Service Level Agreements with suppliers are also called Operating Level Agreements or OLAs.

Communications

Communication with customers is vital so you need to be able to deliver information and receive feedback. Tell your customers what you do, when you do it and how well you do it. Actively solicit feedback. Make sure you know from your customers how well you are doing.

Handling complaints

You will not be able to please everyone all of the time. Your staff will make mistakes. Unforeseen problems will occur, customers will complain. Develop a complaints process, adhere to it and learn from it. A good complaint handling process relies on training staff to use it properly. You should also observe the following:

1. Treat every complaint as a high priority.
2. Make sure you understand what the complaint is and

Customer Details	Supplier Details
Name	Name
Address	Address
Telephone	Telephone

Period of Service from: dd/mm/yy to: dd/mm/yy

Provision of problem call answering

This section gives the title of the service

Details *This section details the service to task level and give estimates of the volume of work expected*

Answer calls – It is anticipated that there will be 50 calls per day.

Log details and provide customer with a reference number.

Refer call to local engineer

Track call

Close call

Performance Standards

This section details the expected performance of the supplier at task level

98% of calls to be answered within 5 rings

100% of callers to receive a reference number

80% of calls to be referred to local engineer within 30 minutes

100% of calls to be transferred to engineers within 1 hour of receipt

Call history to be maintained including customer call backs

Cost of Service

Penalties

This section details any penalties that might be incurred by non-performance

Refund of 20% of fees if performance standards fall below agreed level on three consecutive months on a rolling month basis.

Date of Review

Quarterly reviews

Signed for Customer _____

Signed for Supplier _____

collect the information in such a way that anyone who has to speak to this customer about their complaint has all the information in front of them. Don't antagonise your customer further by making them retell their experience over and over again. They will get angrier with each retelling.

3. Apologise and mean it.
4. Act on the complaint – some problems will require you to chase other people; others will require action in form of recompense, refunds or other appropriate measures. Make sure everyone who handles complaints knows what they are empowered to do. If you are not prepared to empower your help desk staff to resolve complaints, make sure only senior staff or yourself handles them.
5. Don't keep making the same mistakes over and over again. Review the complaints that have been made and act to stop them happening again.

Difficult customers

Every help desk has a few of these. There is no simple routine to placate them but there are a few basic rules.

- Stay polite and calm
- Listen to what they have to say and try to resolve the problem. If you have authority and resources to achieve what they ask, do it – but not at the expense of other more urgent customers
- Never promise anything you cannot deliver – they will be even more unhappy later

Summary

By now, you should know who your customers are and what you are delivering to them. If you feel you are trying to achieve the impossible with too few resources, take a little time to assess the main issues:

- Too few staff – think about recruiting more, looking for opportunities to modify the service, renegotiating the service levels
- Not enough time to act on the lists of things you have decided you need to do – determine what is important and do those first. If every thing is important just deal with one thing at a time
- If customer service standards need a bit of work, invest in some training
- Whatever you do, enlist the support of your customers, tell them your plans but make sure they are realistic

Communication – keeping everyone informed

Today we will look at the major methods of communication, tell you why you need to use them in the help desk and give you some basic guidelines for communicating successfully.

- Meetings
- Reports
- Presentations
- Publicity
- Telephone
- Gossip

Meetings

The help desk manager should hold or attend the following meetings on a regular basis:

- Review meetings with customers and service suppliers – use your measurement data to back up your discussions
- Team meetings with staff
- Negotiation meetings with customers and service suppliers. How well are they doing? What information and measurements do you want?
- Progress meetings with management – don't forget the measurement
- Project meetings relating to new systems and services

How to hold an effective meeting.

1 Has your meeting got a purpose – make sure you know why you are meeting and what you want to achieve.

2 Set a time, book a room, set a time limit, the shorter the better. No meeting should be more than two hours in length. People won't attend if they get bored, so it is better to hold two or three short meetings on each main topic.

3 Decide who needs to be there, if you need a decision-maker or information about a particular subject make sure the relevant people are there. If they cannot attend, it is more effective to delay the meeting by a day or two to make sure all the attendees can get there. If the topic is very important, issue a reminder the day before. If a key person wants to send a deputy, check that the individual has authority to act.

4 Prepare an agenda and circulate it to the attendees. Be prepared to answer questions about the agenda before the meeting. On your copy, note down the outcome you would like from the discussion and impose a time limit on the discussion.

5 Prepare for the meeting, gather all the information, summarise the key points, prepare and back up any arguments make notes.
6 Start on time and **stick to the agenda**. Make sure you chair your meeting. Keep an eye on the time; if discussions go round in circles, ask for a decision or suspend discussion until the end of the meeting. Move on to the next point. Make notes or appoint someone to take minutes. At the end of the meeting go back to unfinished topics. If no decision can be reached, tell the attendees to find an answer and set a new date for a short meeting. Summarise the main points and decisions of the meeting and then close or set a date for next meeting and close.

Within twenty-four hours write up the minutes or a summary of the meeting and circulate it to all attendees and any other interested parties.

How to attend meetings effectively
1 Do you need to attend? Are you the right person to make the decision that may be wanted? Are you the most knowledgeable about the subject? If the answer is 'no' tell the organiser of the meeting so that they can invite the right person.
2 If you don't know why you are being invited to the meeting – ask!
Prepare for the meeting – if you have points you need to get across, write them down. Take supporting documents (enough copies for other attendees, if appropriate).
3 Don't follow the herd – if you object to something say so, make sure your objection is noted and why, even if you are outvoted. Issues are often agreed upon because no

one is prepared to speak out, but it often only takes one person to express concerns for others to find their misgivings as well.

4 Don't behave badly if you are outvoted, and be prepared to accept other points of view – especially if you are the boss.

Reports

A report is your opportunity to deliver facts and conclusions in a self-contained way, but all too often the report writer loses the opportunity through badly-constructed reports.

The help desk manager will probably need to prepare the following reports.

> * Monthly service delivery reports – containing details of how the help desk has performed
> * Incident reports – information about major problems
> * Business cases
> * Proposals to take on additional services – new services require planning
> * Project implementation reviews – gives valuable feedback as to what happened when a project went live

Many of these reports will include factual data including measurement of performance.

When writing reports, avoid waffle, use simple language (if you must use jargon explain it in a glossary) and stick to the facts. All reports follow a basic structure which can be adapted to your needs.

Index/contents	Useful in describing where all the information lies
Management summary	Either a short paragraph or up to three or four pages long. It tells senior managers who are short of time the main points in the report. They are often presented as a series of bullet points covering each main section. It should be a precis of the report and not straight copies of sections or paragraphs of the main report
Acknowledgements	Who helped or contributed?
Introduction	Why the report has been written, what it contains and who has prepared it
Background	Sometimes incorporated into the introduction, but in longer reports a detailed history or scene setting information is valuable
Methodology	Not always necessary but is useful if the report is describing an activity that was carried out, for example a review or a process
Findings	Contains all the relevant data and information, or a summary of it. Data may be in tables that should form the appendices to the report
Conclusions	It is important to refer back to the relevant supporting information. In a short report this section may be amalgamated with the findings or the recommendations
Recommendations	The suggested actions based on the findings and conclusions
Bibliography	Mostly used in academic reports and details the original source of supporting documents or literature by author, title and date

| Glossary | Appears at the beginning or end, and contains an explanation of technical terms and jargon |
| Appendices | Contain data, graphs performance measurement and supporting documentation |

Presentations

The help desk manager is often called upon to present information to others. If you need to convince your boss of something, present information to your organisation or tell your team about a new process, the following points will help.

Preparation
1 Decide what you need to say:
 – set it out one point at a time in a logical order;
 – write it out in note form or put it on cue cards.
2 Prepare slides, flip charts, models or any other visual aids:
 – make them readable;
 – simple (one idea to a page);
 – no more than five points supporting it (use continuation pages if necessary);
 – keep them in step with your notes or cue cards.

Practise
1 Go through your presentation and time it. Allow time for questions.
2 Practise it at least three times on your own and say it out loud.
3 Revise it if necessary.
4 Practise it again in front of a friendly critic – some one you trust who will tell you where it needs polish.
5 Practise it again – by this time you will know it quite well.

On the day

1 Get everything ready before you start, make sure everything works.
2 Make sure you have a drink of water if your mouth dries or you need a few seconds to think. Having a few sips of water will give you that time.
3 Check that everyone can hear you when you make your introductions.
4 Speak clearly and try not to rush. Even if your voice and hand shake, if you have practiced you will know the presentation and it will run smoothly.

Don't

1 Ask someone else to prepare for you.
2 Think that you can get by without preparation, practise or visual aids.
3 Crack jokes.

Publicity

Why advertise? The help desk needs publicity if it is to be used effectively and there are two points to make:

1. What you should say

- What service you provide:
  hours of operation, what you can do
- How to contact you:
  phone, e-mail etc plus details of what you want from each caller: name number etc.
- How effective you are:
  How many calls did you resolve last week? What is the average call resolution time? What were the major problems? Why did they happen? What have you done about it?
- Special messages:
  Special advice such as new viruses, system downtime
- How to complain:
  No one gets things right all the time. Give a clear complaints mechanism and then your customers won't invent their own

2. Where you should say it

- Notice boards:
  Your organisation probably has notice boards sited at strategic points in the building. Take advantage of these but make sure you keep the information up to date.

- Newsletters:
  Appoint someone to edit this. Make it a manageable size – two or four sides of A4 depending on your printing capability should be plenty. Make sure it contains interesting information. IT projects, performance statistics graphically presented, hints and tips or news about members of the team. Distribute monthly or quarterly.
- Circulars:
  These are one-pagers dedicated to a specific topic. They should be used to publicise a new service or to inform about an aspect of the help desk. These need to be prepared with care and should not be overused or they will be binned without being read.
- Internal information systems:
  Use whatever mechanisms are relevant. Some organisations have an in-house magazine, some have briefing sessions, some rely on cascades. If you need to get a message to the entire organisation, use the internal mechanism – provided it works.

Internet/intranet

If your organisation communicates through the web, ensure that the help desk has at least a page describing the services it has to offer. There are other opportunities, including publishing solutions to problems, giving the answers to common or frequently asked questions (FAQs) and enabling the automatic logging of problems. Whatever use you make of the Internet, make sure it is well designed, easy to use, and easy to read.

Telephone

Most of your work is done over the telephone so use it
effectively.

- Treat phone calls you make like a meeting. Plan what
  you are going to say, say it, take note of the responses
- Phone calls you receive contain many messages –
  learn to sort out whether they require actions,
  instructions or information (given or sought)

Gossip

Don't ignore gossip – the informal message may be more
serious than it first appears – it means that someone is clearly
concerned about something. Having mentioned it to you it is
unlikely they will make any formal request for assistance etc,
but if you forget all about it, they will feel let down.

Underlying any office gossip may be something that affects
your part of the organisation. For example, if you hear a
rumour about redundancies and your team is responsible for
allocating system access rights, the secrecy surrounding such
decisions could mean that essential processes like disabling
access rights get forgotten. Discreet enquiries, even if they
lead to denial, might jog memories about essential tasks.

Summary

Today we looked at the importance of good communication,
ranging from formal reports and meetings to informal,
maybe seemingly unimportant, gossip. After all, if you don't
communicate effectively or keep people fully informed, how
can you expect people to know what is expected of them?

Measurement – proving your worth

There is a well known saying that is regularly quoted at
managers: 'If you can't measure it you aren't managing it'.
Managing a help desk is no exception and today we are
going to look at:

- What you should be measuring
- Why you should be measuring it
- Techniques you can use to measure effectively

There are three categories of measurement within the help
desk: staff performance, workload and customer satisfaction.

Staff performance

Performance monitoring tells the help desk manager four
things:

1. How many calls each member of the team is handling
   which, in turn, give a clear indication of the total number
   of calls the help desk can adequately manage in a day

IF YOU CAN'T MEASURE IT
YOU'RE NOT MANAGING IT

2. How long each call takes. Does one operator spend more time on calls than the others? Why? Are they inexperienced or do they spend more time on customer satisfaction?
3. How much of the time is spent actually on the phone or are staff spending more time on other service tasks.
4. The quality of the work carried out by the help desk staff.

Armed with this information the help desk manager can ensure that staff are properly trained, that there are enough staff to do the work and that the priority tasks are the ones that are receiving the most attention. The general assumption is that staff will be performing as well as they are able, but there are sometimes occasions when a staff member is not working as well as the others because they are lazy, or incompetent. Use your organisation's disciplinary process to manage this, but use the data you have collected to support your actions.

Collecting this information relies on the tools that you use. At a very basic level, the telephone system will tell you how many calls you take and how long each call lasts. By analysing this data at extension number level, you will get an idea of each operator's performance.

If you have an ACD, the information is much clearer and more easily extracted. Each member of staff is identifiable to the ACD system and their activity can be recorded, such as how long they took to answer, how long they spent on the call and how long they took to wrap up after the call. This information is valuable for improving response times and identifying training needs.

The call logging software will also contain some call handling information; who the operator was, the time the call was logged, whether it was resolved at once or was passed to some one else to solve, how long the call was open/took to solve.

By looking at the information put into the software, it is possible to assess the quality of the operator's questioning skills and their technical knowledge. If you have voice recording technology, this may also be used to assess the quality of operator performance. Randomly select calls and listen to them, making sure that the call is handled in the agreed manner for your organisation.

Workload

Measuring workload, that is numbers, distribution, types, and resolution of calls and problems, is probably the most important set of measures to get to grips with because these define where the organisation should devote its problem-solving energies. In addition, if you don't know what your workload is, you can't budget effectively.

Call statistics
How many calls and when they are received determines staffing levels. There are three groups of statistics that illustrate this.

1. Call distribution on a 'normal day' is measured by counting the number of calls in each agreed segment of time, usually 15 or 30 minute intervals throughout the day. As you can see from graph 1, the call pattern in most help desks shows a double peak, with most calls

occurring between 9.30 a.m. and 11.00 a.m. or between 2.00 p.m. and 3.30 p.m.

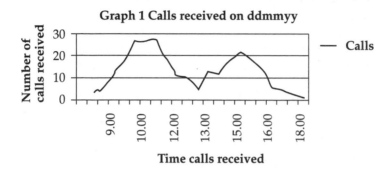

2. Call distribution on a day in which a crisis occurs is clearly illustrated in graph 2 by the very high peak in the late morning. The twin peaks of the normal day have flattened out but are still there.

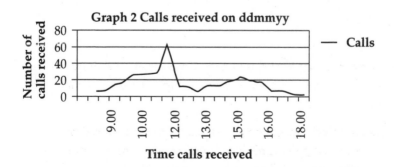

These graphs can be combined and plotted over time to show call distribution over weeks or months. Most organisations have a working cycle that can be monitored in terms of calls received. An accounts-driven help desk may have high peaks at the end of each month, with very high activity in April and May. A manufacturer with a twelve-week production process may have four defined cycles throughout the year. The raw statistics from these graphs will give you an idea of when you should provide cover for the desk. This data was collected from the telephone statistics.

3. Similar graphs plotted for the abandoned call rate show how many people attempted to call the help desk but gave up because the lines were too busy or the wait was too long.

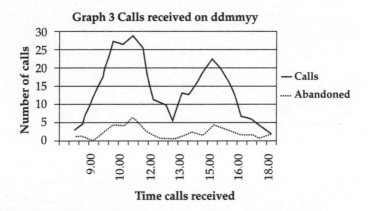

Graph 3 Calls received on ddmmyy

A lot of attention is paid to abandoned call rates because they are evidence that the customer is getting irritated. The average rate across the help desk industry is about 7% of all calls. If the rate in your organisation is substantially higher, it is important to look at the reasons why.

- The help desk might be understaffed. If so, the measurements will show all staff on the phone most, if not all, of the time and no other service tasks will be completed. Alternatively, staff may be on the phone for short periods as other measured tasks are taking priority.
- There may be a serious problem that is increasing call volumes beyond predicted levels. For example, a product may be sold for which one of the operating instructions may be confusing or complex. If it is a high-volume product, there will be a lot of calls until the problem is identified and rectified.
- If abandoned call rates are high only at peak times, it means that the resources need to be reorganised to cope. A word of warning here! It is tempting to just make more people available to answer the phone. If you do this without paying attention to how the calls are handled or resolved further down the line, you are simply moving the problem from one area to another.

Problem management relies on information about the problems. When logging problems you need to break them down into types. How many types of call you have will depend upon your help desk function but you should be able to log every call you receive as either a new incident or problem, or as a follow up call to an existing incident or problem.

By categorising the logged calls you will soon know what the top five reasons for calling your help desk are. Problem management means looking at the underlying cause of

those problems and rectifying them. If your help desk serves the general public, product issues and problems will generate calls and when the issue is resolved the calls will go away, only to be replaced by something else. If your help desk serves your organisation, there may be some problems that will remain consistently in the top five. For example, where the help desk sets security passwords, resetting them will be a regular activity unless you can improve human memory.

In order to reduce the calls, anything you can do to prevent the calls in the first place is valuable. To do this you must know what problems you are dealing with and be able to act on the information.

Measuring how long callers have to wait for a solution to their problem is also essential, particularly where there are service level agreements in place. If you agree to answer a call within ten seconds and resolve the problem within ten minutes, the opportunities to measure this must be there. Clocks within call logging systems and the software

available within telephone and ACD systems provide the
tools; it is up to you to use them.

Crisis reporting

When things go wrong, everyone knows. By using the
measurement opportunities available, you can estimate how
many people were affected, what went wrong, and what
was done to correct the problem. Organisations have this
information but often fail to share it with their customers
who get very cross when they have no idea of what went
wrong or why.

Customer satisfaction

Help desks are usually set up to solve customer problems
and it is important to ensure that the customer is getting
value from the service. However, you are unlikely to
receive huge amounts of praise from your customers.
Remember, when they come to you they are already
unhappy because something has gone wrong. Whatever it
is, they want it fixed 'now', and no matter how well trained
everyone is there will always be calls that can't be solved
first time. However, if you say you will fix 80% of calls first
time, you must be prepared to show that you do (or don't).
The first measure of customer satisfaction comes from the
information you give them about the service you provide.
Measuring customer satisfaction is based on qualitative
measurements and includes:

1 Follow up QA calls

Different organisations have different ways of handling
these. Some help desks routinely call back 5% of all callers
and assess how the call was handled by means of a very
quick on line questionnaire. Others will send out

questionnaires to about 5% of customers seeking feedback. The questionnaires should be short – no more than five questions – and relevant. Questions should relate to a recent call about the service offered, and can be an effective way of regularly assessing performance. However, beware of irritating very regular customers with too many surveys. The results of these surveys should be published in your monthly report/statistics.

2 Performance surveys
These are usually carried out annually, sent to all users of the service and are much more detailed. You should expect to cover all services provided and all aspects of the service. Response to these more detailed surveys should be voluntary and if you are lucky in excess of 30% will be returned. Don't be surprised if you get a lot less but do encourage your customers to respond either with a prize (if budgets allow) or reminders (if possible).

Make sure you have an easy to use mechanism for analysing the results. If you have the budget, it is often worthwhile employing specialists to do this for you but check that you have clearly explained what you want and how you want the results presented. Publish the results of the survey to your customers. The survey should not only confirm what you know about the service you give but also show what else your customers want from the service. Use the results to plan your objectives for the next year.

Choosing which measurements to take

If you have a service level agreement with your customers, you must take the measurements of that service. Go back to

Wednesday's section on service level agreements and how to define measures. If you have no formal service level agreements, it is still worth measuring and reporting how well you are doing – it helps manage customer expectations. At the very minimum you should expect to report on:

- The number of calls received in the month
- The number resolved within ten minutes or at first point of contact
- The percentage or number resolved within the service level
- The level of satisfaction of the customers
- Details of any major incidents that occurred in the month and what effect it had and what was done about it

Staff performance needs to be measured for appraisal purposes but these measurements can also form part of incentive schemes such as employee of the month. You need to routinely record:

- The number of calls handled
- Average time spent on each call
- Quality of call handling

Even if you have no staff appraisal mechanism, knowledge of how people are performing will allow you to give appropriate feedback and if necessary training. Information about the calls you take will help you adjust the service to your customers so that it remains appropriate. Go back to Sunday. Look at the service you are providing and add a column to Table 2 on page 12. Decide on the relevant measures to take.

Practical Considerations
Choose measurements that you can actually measure.
Details such as number of calls per day are usually quite
easy to record. Measuring the number of calls that are
abandoned within ten seconds may be more difficult if you
don't have a reasonably sophisticated telephone system or
ACD.

- Choose measurements that are relevant. Your ACD
  may give you a breakdown of call abandonment
  rates at ten-second intervals but you are probably
  only interested in three statistics:
  – what proportion of calls are abandoned;
  – how many calls are abandoned after hearing a
    service message (count these as answered calls);
  – what is the average time before calls are
    abandoned? Compare this to the average
    answering time. If the former is shorter than the
    latter you have irritated customers.
- Put your measurement results into an easy-to-follow
  format: graphs, pictures, charts, etc. No one wants
  to interpret pages and pages of numeric data.

Summary

Keep your measurements simple but accurate. All of the
measurements you take will be wasted unless you do
something with them. Use Thursday's work on
communication for ways and means of presenting all this
data, and make sure someone is skilled in producing
meaningful graphs and charts. Use the data itself to support
your actions.

Finding time and reviewing progress

Today we are going to look at time management and at reviewing progress.

First we will cover the time management topics.

- Where does the day go?
- Assessing priorities
- Delegation

Then we will look at the review topics:

- Reporting progress
- Health checks
- Getting more budget
- Where to get help

Where does the day go

First you must find out how you spend your time. We are back once again to writing down what you do for every minute of every day for at least a week – preferably two or three. The table on page 82 shows you the kind of information to include. Make sure you complete your analysis in a reasonable amount of detail.

	Monday	Tuesday	Wednesday
08 00	Arrive log on, coffee		
08 15	Attend weekend review meeting		
08.30			
08 45	Speak to team individually		
09 00	e-mail		
09 15	Prepare monthly		
09 30	stats		
09 45	+ 3 calls 2 mins each		
10 00	Loo, coffee		
10 15	Progress meeting		
10 30			
10 45	Saw Phil, talked about system		
11 00			

If you are conscientious about doing this, you will produce
an analysis that may look a little like the one below.

Analysis

1. Total hours spent at work ☐
2. Time spent on staff management ☐
3. Telephone calls ☐
4. e-mail ☐
5. Meetings ☐
6. Project work ☐
7. Miscellaneous ☐
8. Personal ☐

Structuring your day

Look at the pattern of each day.

- Are there any trends – could you merge some activities or move them to make better use of time?
- Look at each specific activity – was it necessary?
- Is it part of what you should be doing?
- How many interruptions were there in project activities?

Finding more time

Plan each day the day before. Allocate a time to each specific task and stick to it.

Set the priorities on each task so that if something goes wrong you know what you can leave till later. All of the following activities will help you to regain time.

- Plan meetings – look at Thursday again
- Allow yourself 'do not disturb' time. Use this time to achieve priority tasks. However, the most time you can allow for this is two hours, although if this is

strictly observed, you will achieve huge amounts in
that time.

- Keep a list of unscheduled activities that you do as
  a favour or because the last caller asked you to.
  Assess what you should be doing and what you
  should delegate.
  Keep telephone calls to the point – plan them like a
  meeting.
- Look at the things that never get done and ask
  yourself why?
  - Are they too difficult? Seek help
  - Don't you want to do them? Just do them
  - Are they unimportant? Don't do them
- Review what you do each day and how long it
  takes. You will get better at estimating tasks and
  setting deadlines

If you do not believe how you consume time, take a look at the time stealers.

Time stealers

- Procrastination is the thief of time – if you are tidying your desk because you don't want to start work, take a look at what you are doing.
- The boss – 'Have you got a minute?' The answer need not always be yes. It should be, 'Is it urgent? Can I come and see you when I have finished this? If it's reasonable to wait, the boss will wait.
- Staff who can't/won't act without authority. This means you have got some training to do – put it on the list.
- Maisie from accounts – she always has a problem that only you can solve. Is that true? Persuade her to call the help desk number next time.
- John from the golf club about next month's games. An amazing amount of social activity can intrude on to the working day. Arrange to meet John for lunch.
- The chocolate machine /cigarette breaks. The chocolate machine and the smoking zone always seem to be a long way from your bit of the office. Keep an eye on the time you and your staff spend there.

How to deal with a crisis

The other activity that takes a significant amount of a help desk manager's time is coping with crises. Even this can be made more manageable by the following activities:

- Note the times when your organisation has critical activities, for example, year-end accounting. Have you made sure that you have got access to extra staff at this time and have you discussed with the departments involved an order of priority of any potential problems? Have you vetoed any planned changes to their systems during this time?
- Make a list of who does what when a crisis occurs, instead of people relying on you to delegate activities.
- Make a contingency plan – when things go very seriously wrong do you have an alternative set of options that can be called in? Does this mean diverting all calls to another area or activating back

up systems or moving everything to another site? Is the option available and have you tested to see whether or not it will work?

- Reschedule low priority work – if you have prioritised the activities within the help desk, you know what you can defer until after the crisis is over.
- Look at the underlying reasons for each crisis and see if they can be avoided in the future. Is the organisation's change management process effective? Have all steps been taken to avoid problems with new processes, products, systems and procedures?

Even if you have taken all reasonable steps to manage a crisis they will continue to occur, but they will be seen as a blip rather than wholesale disaster.

JUST COVERING ALL
ANGLES...

Assessing priorities

Prioritisation tells everyone what should be done first. If the low priorities never get done, they are either not worth doing or you have insufficient resource to complete all the required activities. Set priorities for all activities and let your customers know what to expect.

Deciding what is important

- There are some activities which are seen to be important and never questioned. Check the importance of these so-called priority activities. What do they contribute to customers, the business, to profits?
- Are some people more important than others? Why? Should work for them have a higher priority?
- What are your organisation's main functions or objectives? If the task does not contribute to these, is it a high priority?
- What would happen if it didn't get done? Do some impact analysis – this means thinking about what would be affected, what else wouldn't happen, what problems would occur, would it really affect customers, business or profits.
- How many people are affected? One or a thousand?

To each of the above questions you can assign a scoring mechanism. Keep it simple:

0 = no effect 1 = low effect 2 = medium effect 3 = high effect.

If you score 10 or more, the task is important; less than 4 and it is not.

- If you briefly assess each task against the questions above and score them, you will get a good idea of what is really important.
- Keep a list of the top five ongoing tasks for you and for your team.
- Inevitably there will be one-off emergencies and your ability to handle these will depend on the day. Assess everything and tell your customer how you have reached your assessment. Be prepared to discuss and, if necessary, say no to unreasonable requests.

Dealing with conflicts

Sometimes your customer is going to be very unhappy; sometimes the customer will also be your boss.

- Use the current list of priorities and ask why this particular task is more important than the ones you have.
- Discuss whether another task should move down the list of priorities. Explain the impact of doing that task. Is it still necessary to do it now or can it wait or can someone else do it?
- Sometimes you won't have a choice and the best you can do is reassess the list and advise the people who are affected by the change of it.

- Don't be influenced by friendship or threats – both
  will undermine your credibility as a competent
  manager. Threats will be empty if you have made
  your case well.

Delegation

There are good reasons for learning to delegate successfully:

- It gives others a chance to learn about the next step
  in the career ladder and how to handle more
  complex tasks under the guidance of a competent
  manager.
- You give yourself more time to devote to new issues
  and getting to grips with improving the functions that
  your department carries out.
- People learn to trust each other.

Part of the trick of successful delegation is knowing when
to delegate and this includes:

- When. It is easy to fall into the trap of doing a simple
  task because you are able, but if it is not your job you
  should delegate it to the right person. In the scheme
  of customer service ideals this doesn't sit comfortably
  for two reasons. Firstly, the person doesn't know
  whose job it is, so you have a communication
  problem; and secondly, you are working within your
  team and not actually managing it.

- When you want someone else to gain experience as part of a training plan.
- Giving others the opportunity to do something different, something that empowers them or assigns responsibility – it can be a strong motivator.

Only use upward delegation when the task is not appropriate for you. If you need help to do it, and if it is part of your training, you shouldn't attempt to delegate upwards – you should seek guidance.

When your team attempt to delegate upwards only take those occasional tasks that are inappropriate to them. Use the others as a training opportunity, even if you have to monitor progress and give advice at regular intervals. The next time they will manage the task better.

Reporting progress

An important part of management is knowing what you have achieved and telling people what you have done. A useful tactic to employ is the gathering of key points from regular reports.

If you are managing an existing help desk, produce a document that states where you are now, warts and all. On Sunday you spent time assessing what your help desk does. Use that information. Include a section on your plans for improvement over the next three six and twelve months.

Similarly, if you are starting a help desk set out your aims. Nothing much will change in three months; at the end of six months there should be visible improvement; at the end of a year you should be planning the next set of improvements.

Over the next few months track your progress against that original document, using the reports that you have decided are appropriate to back up the progress you have made.

Don't worry if you have to change your plans; you will be able to explain the reasons behind this. Don't worry if to start with things seem to get worse, it takes time for people to learn new ways. Do worry if the situation continues to deteriorate. It is a sign that you need to change your tactics.

By tracking progress you will be able to demonstrate to your boss and the rest of the organisation just how much things have changed for the better. If, after a few months, nothing has improved, you should have the evidence of insufficient resources and an idea of where additional resources need to be employed, and whether you need people or tools to make the improvements you planned at the outset. In addition, if there have been major failures, admit to them, explain why they occurred and what has been done to prevent recurrences.

Each major project completed should be celebrated with at least an announcement. Keep the top priorities as high profile. Educate your customers as to what is and isn't important in the scheme of things. Let them know when the less important things get done. Show that you are not lurching from crisis to crisis. Communicate!

Health checks

Some organisations like to review their help desks and

compare them with those of other organisations. There are a number of organisations that can do this for which they will charge a fee, and from which you will get a report that advises you where to concentrate your efforts. If you do not have the time to assess your help desk, a health check may be a cost-effective answer but make sure you discuss and document with the consultant what you require and the objectives you need to achieve.

The following statistics are industry standards and are drawn from a recent help desk benchmarking report produced by Help Desk Institute (HDI) (their address is included in the list of useful contacts at the end of the book). Use these statistics as a baseline for assessing your own help desk's current performance:

- The average number of calls handled by each help desk analyst is 32
- The average percentage of abandoned calls is 7.3%
- The average percentage of calls resolved at first level is 64%.

Increasing your budget

Despite your best efforts, there are times when you cannot make progress unless you get more budget or resources. You cannot rely on a 'gut feel' to get more money – you need to prove a business case. Use your measurements to build the case and plan the improvement project in advance, costing accurately each step.

New members of staff don't just have salary costs, they have training needs, recruitment costs, equipment and office space and the process takes time. The time budget also needs to be calculated. If you can't recruit for three months and it takes two months to train effectively you won't begin to realise any benefits at all for six months.

The number of calls multiplied by the average length of call tells what resources you need today. You also need to show that call numbers are increasing or that other work is making demands on time. Each new project adds work load – calculate how much. Be realistic about problem management and how effective call reduction efforts have been. Prepare alternative scenarios, more sophisticated tools compared with fewer staff, or a reduction in service level compared with an increase in staff.

Ask your finance team what information is required when presenting your business case. Don't be fobbed off with a request for a list of 'cost v. benefits'. Make sure the finance department shows you the effect of discounted cash flows and how to assess the true value of benefits. Intangible benefits are usually ignored by accountants but they often add a competitive edge so find the strategy expert in your company to discuss this with.

Present your business case clearly and to the right people – you need to get the financial decision-makers on board. Make sure the consequences of not making the improvements are real and known. When you receive the extra funding, make sure you don't overspend and that you really do measure the benefits gained.

Change

As well as managing your help desk, you also have to keep

up with changes. Regular meetings with other managers and project leaders will allow you to plan and implement new services and arrange training. Everything that happens in your organisation will either directly or indirectly affect the help desk. Make sure you know what is going on by reviewing corporate plans and attending *relevant* meetings and briefings. Anticipate what the help desk will need to do and prepare for it.

Finally, you might feel that you will never achieve everything you want to with your help desk because there is so much change, which is happening so quickly, but this should not discourage you from wanting to try. Success will come from knowing what is wanted, what you need to do to get there and communicating effectively. Enjoy the challenge!

Where to get help

Here is a list of useful names and addresses of organisations that contribute to the help desk industry.

Help Desk Institute
21 High Street
Green Street Green
Orpington,
Kent
Tel +44(0)1689 862999
E-mail: info@hdi-europe.com

Pink Roccade
County House
17 Friar Street
Reading
Berks RG1 1DB
Tel +44(0)118 951 9600

IT Infrastructure Library
ITSMF Ltd.
1a Taverners Square,
Silver Road,
Norwich NR3 4SY
Tel: +44(0)1603 767181

Jacqueline Chapman (Consultant)
Westfield House,
Gidding Road.
Sawtry
Cambs PE17 5UJ
Tel +44(0)1487 832941
E-mail: JacquieChapman@aol.com